D1053102

JUST DAUGHTERS

JUST DAUGHTERS

The Adorable, Incorrigible, Wonder of Girls

Melissa Sovey

Willow Creek Press®

Published by Willow Creek Press, Inc.
P.O. Box 147, Minocqua, Wisconsin 54548

Photo Credits: p2 © Greg Stott/Masterfile; p7 © Minden Pictures/Masterfile;
p8 © Mike & Lisa Husar/www.teamhusar.com; p11 © Mike & Lisa Husar/www.teamhusar.com;
p12 © Chris Hendrickson/Masterfile; p15 © Minden Pictures/Masterfile; p16 © Minden Pictures/Masterfile;
p19 © Minden Pictures/Masterfile; p20 © Richard Stacks/www.kimballstock.com;
p23 © Minden Pictures/Masterfile; p24 © Mike & Lisa Husar/www.teamhusar.com;
p27 © Frank Krahmer/Masterfile; p28 © Klein-Hubert/www.kimballstock.com;
p31 © Richard Stacks/www.kimballstock.com; p32 © Minden Pictures/Masterfile;
p35 © Gary Randall/www.kimballstock.com; p36 © Minden Pictures/Masterfile;
p39 © Mike & Lisa Husar/www.teamhusar.com; p40 © Minden Pictures/Masterfile;
p43 © Minden Pictures/Masterfile; p44 © Minden Pictures/Masterfile;
p47 © Kitchin & Hurst/www.kimballstock.com; p48 © Nick Ridley/www.kimballstock.com;
p51 © Mike & Lisa Husar/www.teamhusar.com; p52 © Wildlife GmbH/www.kimballstock.com;
p55 © Mike & Lisa Husar/www.teamhusar.com; p56 © Gerard Lacz/www.kimballstock.com;
p59 © Mike & Lisa Husar/www.teamhusar.com; p60 © Steven Kazlowski/www.kimballstock.com;
p63 © Mike & Lisa Husar/www.teamhusar.com; p64 © Keith Neale/Masterfile;
p67 © Minden Pictures/Masterfile; p68 © Mike & Lisa Husar/www.teamhusar.com;
p71 © Klein-Hubert/www.kimballstock.com; p72 © Mike & Lisa Husar/www.teamhusar.com;
p75 © Minden Pictures/Masterfile; p76 © Mike & Lisa Husar/www.teamhusar.com;
p79 © Wildlife GmbH/www.kimballstock.com; p83 © Mike & Lisa Husar/www.teamhusar.com;
p84 © Scanpix Creative/Masterfile; p87 © Gary Randall Photography/www.kimballstock.com;
p88 © Daniel J. Cox/www.kimballstock.com; p91 © Winter-Churchill/www.kimballstock.com;
p92 © Daniel J. Cox/www.kimballstock.com; p95 © Ron Kimball/www.kimballstock.com

Design: Donnie Rubo
Printed in Canada

A FEW FACTS
ABOUT GIRLS

❧❦❧

"Girls are giggles with freckles all over them."

—*Author Unknown*

❧

"Little girls are the nicest things that happen to people.
They are born with a little bit of angel shine about
them, and though it wears thin sometimes there
is always enough left to lasso your heart."

—*Alan Marshall Beck*

ᏪᏫᏪᏫ

"A daughter is a treasure—
and a cause of sleeplessness."

—*Ben Sirach*

❦

"A girl is Innocence playing in the mud, Beauty
standing on its head, and Motherhood
dragging a doll by the foot."

—*Alan Marshall Beck*

❦

"Little girls were meant to be snuggled
and smothered with affection. They
are irresistible magnets for cuddles."

—*Melissa Sovey*

❦

"Biologically speaking, if something bites
you it's more likely to be female."

—*Desmond Morris*

ભજ✦ᏆᏫ

"A little girl is sugar and spice and everything nice—especially when she's taking a nap."

—*Unknown*

〜〜✣〜〜

"In every girl is a goddess."

—*Francesca Lia Block*

∾⧫∾

"Never underestimate the fierceness of a little girl challenged to a wrestling match."

—*Melissa Sovey*

❧

"A daughter is the happy memories of the past, the joyful moments of the present, and the hope and promise of the future."

—*Unknown*

⤳⤳⚭⤳⤳

"A son is a son till he takes him a wife,
a daughter is a daughter all of her life."

—*Irish Saying*

IN THE BEGINNING...
BABIES AND GIRLHOOD

❧

"Little girls, like butterflies, need no excuse."

—*Robert A. Heinlein*

❧

"When Charles first saw our child Mary, he said all the proper things for a new father. He looked upon the poor little red thing and blurted, 'She's more beautiful than the Brooklyn Bridge.'"

—*Helen Hayes*

❧

"A tiny daughter gives parents a life
in a climate of perpetual wonder."

—*Pierre Doucet*

❦

"A little girl can be sweeter (and badder) oftener than anyone else in the world. She can jitter around, and stomp, and make funny noises that frazzle your nerves, yet just when you open your mouth she stands there demure with that special look in her eyes."

—*Alan Marshall Beck*

"Our daughters are the most precious of our treasures, the dearest possessions of our homes and the objects of our most watchful love."

—*Pierre Doucet*

❧

"Nature makes boys and girls lovely to look upon so they can be tolerated until they acquire some sense."

—*William Lyon Phelps*

"There was a little girl
Who had a little curl
Right in the middle of her forehead;
And when she was good
She was very, very good,
But when she was bad she was horrid."

—*Henry Wadsworth Longfellow*

"A daughter is your greatest source of pride and your greatest hope for the future. The happiest moment of your life was the day she was introduced to the world."

—*Bettie Meschler*

❧

"It is rare that one can see in a little boy the promise of a man, but one can almost always see in a little girl the threat of a woman."

—*Alexandre Dumas*

☙❧

"The most important gift anyone can give a girl
is a belief in her own power as an individual,
her value without reference to gender, her
respect as a person with potential."

—*Emilie Buchwald*

LESSONS FROM OUR DAUGHTERS

❦

"The knowingness of little girls is
hidden underneath their curls."

—*Phyllis McGinley*

—❧—

"The father of a daughter is nothing but a high-class hostage. A father turns a stony face to his sons, berates them, shakes his antlers, paws the ground, snorts, runs them off into the underbrush, but when his daughter puts her arm over his shoulder and says, 'Daddy, I need to ask you something,' he is a pat of butter in a hot frying pan."

—*Garrison Keillor*

ভওক৩ও

"The necessity for extra bathrooms grows exponentially with the number of girls in the house."

—*Melissa Sovey*

❦

"A three year old child is a being who gets almost as much fun out of a fifty-six dollar set of swings as it does out of finding a small green worm."

—*Bill Vaughan*

❦

"There is a garden in her face, where
roses and white lilies blow."

—*Thomas Campion*

༄ ✦ ༄

"I love to see a young girl go out
and grab the world by the lapels."

—*Maya Angelou*

"From the time she was born, until she was fifteen, I didn't know where I left off and she began. We were joined at the hip or the heart or the brain."

—*Lee Grant*

TURNING POINTS...
INTO ADOLESCENCE

❧❦❧

"To an adolescent, there is nothing in the
world more embarrassing than a parent."

—*Dave Barry*

❧

"Any astronomer can predict with absolute accuracy just where every star in the universe will be at 11:30 tonight. He can make no such prediction about his teenage daughter."

—James T. Adams

❧

"Daughters are like flowers, they fill the world with beauty, and sometimes attract pests."

—*Unknown*

"Many a man wishes he were strong enough to tear a telephone book in half—especially if he has a teenage daughter."

—*Guy Lombardo*

"Watching your daughter being collected by her date feels like handing over a million dollar Stradivarius to a gorilla."

—Jim Bishop

꙰

"Be to her virtues very kind;
Be to her faults a little blind."

—*Matthew Prior*

"You have to hang in there, because two or three years later, the gremlins will return your child, and she will be wonderful again."

—*Jill Eikenberry*

AND NOW YOU
ARE GROWN

❧❧❧

"Go girl, seek happy nights to happy days."

—*William Shakespeare*

❧

"You are your child's keeper until she
is mature enough to keep herself."

—*Laura Ramirez*

⚜

"How long is a girl a child? She is a child, and then one morning you wake up and she's a woman, and a dozen different people of whom you recognize none."

—*Louis L'Amour*

❦

"To a father growing old nothing
is dearer than a daughter."

—*Euripides*

"Of all the haunting moments of motherhood,
few rank with hearing your own words come
out of your daughter's mouth."

—*Victoria Secunda*

"And thou shalt in thy daughter see,
This picture, once resembled thee."

—*Ambrose Philips*

❧

"We mothers are learning to mark our mothering success by our daughters' lengthening flight."

—*Letty Cottin Pogrebin*

꧁ ꧂

"There's something like a line of gold thread running through a man's words when he talks to his daughter, and gradually over the years it gets to be long enough for you to pick up in your hands and weave into a cloth that feels like love itself."

—*John Gregory Brown*

❧

"There may not be a finer way for a woman to fully understand the tribulations and triumphs of her life, from youth to adulthood, than by raising a daughter."

—*Melissa Sovey*

"What I wanted most for my daughter was that she be able to soar confidently in her own sky, whatever that may be."

—Helen Claes

Win   unique

SVAD 12/14
MSJ 5/15
RAC 4/17

AL 1/18

AZ 11/18

TLC 1/20